Sara Seager
Planetary Scientist

by Paige V. Polinsky

BLASTOFF! READERS 2

BELLWETHER MEDIA • MINNEAPOLIS, MN

Note to Librarians, Teachers, and Parents:

Blastoff! Readers are carefully developed by literacy experts and combine standards-based content with developmentally appropriate text.

Level 1 provides the most support through repetition of high-frequency words, light text, predictable sentence patterns, and strong visual support.

Level 2 offers early readers a bit more challenge through varied simple sentences, increased text load, and less repetition of high-frequency words.

Level 3 advances early-fluent readers toward fluency through increased text and concept load, less reliance on visuals, longer sentences, and more literary language.

Level 4 builds reading stamina by providing more text per page, increased use of punctuation, greater variation in sentence patterns, and increasingly challenging vocabulary.

Level 5 encourages children to move from "learning to read" to "reading to learn" by providing even more text, varied writing styles, and less familiar topics.

Whichever book is right for your reader, Blastoff! Readers are the perfect books to build confidence and encourage a love of reading that will last a lifetime!

This edition first published in 2019 by Bellwether Media, Inc.

No part of this publication may be reproduced in whole or in part without written permission of the publisher. For information regarding permission, write to Bellwether Media, Inc., Attention: Permissions Department, 6012 Blue Circle Drive, Minnetonka, MN 55343.

Library of Congress Cataloging-in-Publication Data

Names: Polinsky, Paige V., author.
Title: Sara Seager : Planetary Scientist / by Paige V. Polinsky.
Description: Minneapolis, MN : Bellwether Media, Inc., [2019] | Series: Blastoff! Readers. Women Leading the Way | Audience: Ages 5-8. | Audience: K to grade 3. | Includes bibliographical references and index.
Identifiers: LCCN 2018033440 (print) | LCCN 2018034669 (ebook) | ISBN 9781681036687 (ebook) | ISBN 9781626179448 (hardcover : alk. paper) | ISBN 9781618915054 (pbk. : alk. paper)
Subjects: LCSH: Seager, Sara–Juvenile literature. | Planetary scientists–Biography–Juvenile literature. | Astrophysicists–Biography–Juvenile literature. | Women astronomers–Biography–Juvenile literature. | Astronomers–Biography–Juvenile literature. | Extrasolar planets–Juvenile literature. | Outer space–Exploration–Juvenile literature.
Classification: LCC QB46 (ebook) | LCC QB46 .P64 2019 (print) | DDC 523.4092 [B] –dc23
LC record available at https://lccn.loc.gov/2018033440

Text copyright © 2019 by Bellwether Media, Inc. BLASTOFF! READERS and associated logos are trademarks and/or registered trademarks of Bellwether Media, Inc. SCHOLASTIC, CHILDREN'S PRESS, and associated logos are trademarks and/or registered trademarks of Scholastic Inc., 557 Broadway, New York, NY 10012.

Editor: Kate Moening   Designer: Andrea Schneider

Printed in the United States of America, North Mankato, MN.

Table of Contents

Who Is Sara Seager?	4
Getting Her Start	6
Changing the World	12
Sara's Future	18
Glossary	22
To Learn More	23
Index	24

Who Is Sara Seager?

Sara Seager is a **scientist**. She studies **outer space**.

Her work helps people learn about **exoplanets**. She is trying to find one just like Earth!

drawing of an exoplanet

"EVERYTHING BRAVE HAS TO START SOMEWHERE." (2016)

Getting Her Start

Sara was born in Canada. Her parents **divorced** when she was young.

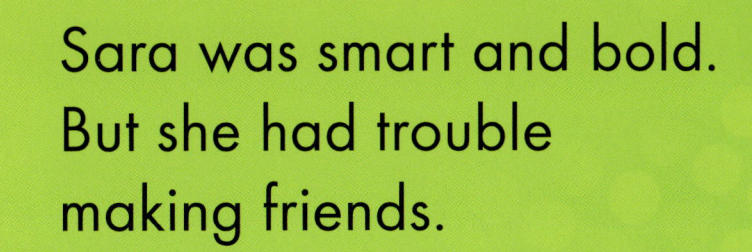

Sara was smart and bold. But she had trouble making friends.

Toronto, Canada

Young Sara was **amazed** by the night sky. At age 16, she learned about **astronomy**.

Sara Seager Profile

Birthday: July 21, 1971
Hometown: Toronto, Canada
Industry: astronomy/education
Education:
- mathematics and physics degrees (University of Toronto)
- astronomy degree (Harvard University)

Influences and Heroes:
- David Seager (father)
- Dimitar Sasselov (scientist; Sara's professor)
- John Bahcall (scientist; Sara's boss at Princeton)
- Charles Beichman (NASA scientist)

Sara dreamed of exploring the stars.

Sara moved to the United States for school. Her father told her to become a doctor.

Sara became a scientist instead.

"THE MOST AMAZING THING TO ME IS JUST **HOW VAST THE UNIVERSE IS.**" (2017)

Changing the World

exoplanet K2-33b, discovered 2016

Exoplanets were discovered while Sara was in school. She began studying them.

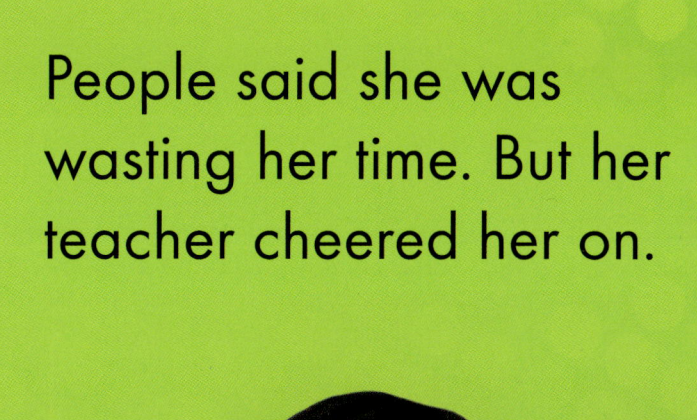

People said she was wasting her time. But her teacher cheered her on.

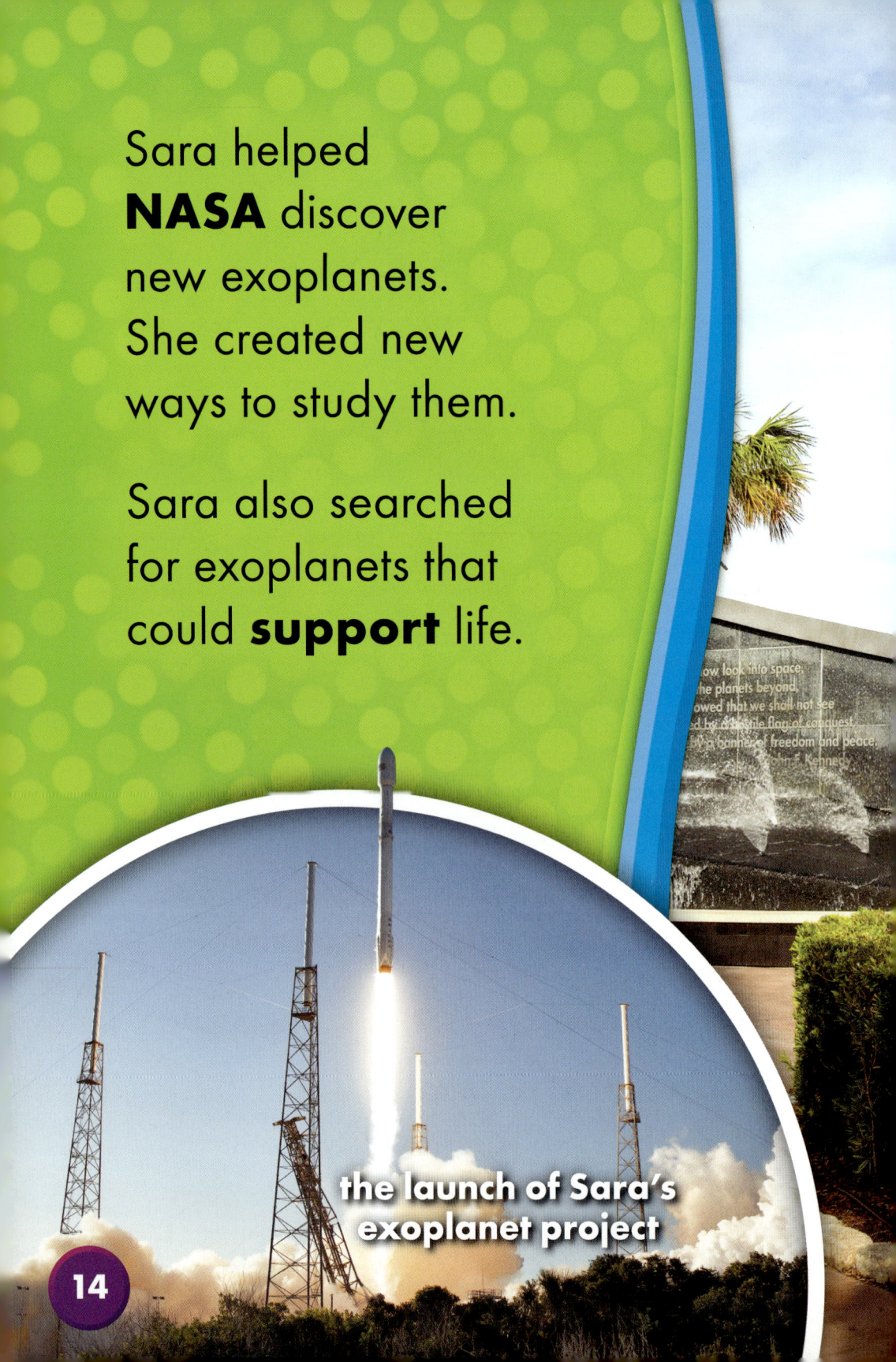

Sara helped **NASA** discover new exoplanets. She created new ways to study them.

Sara also searched for exoplanets that could **support** life.

the launch of Sara's exoplanet project

NASA Space Center (Florida)

Sara's husband cared for their sons. But he got very sick. When he died, Sara was all alone.

exoplanet Kepler-16b, discovered 2011

Sara receiving a grant

Sara won a **grant** for her work. She used it to care for her family.

Sara's Future

Massachusetts Institute of Technology (MIT), where Sara teaches

Today, Sara is leading a NASA project to find new exoplanets. She is also a **professor**.

Sara Seager Timeline

1999 Sara becomes the first person in the U.S. to finish school with a study in exoplanets

2007 Sara becomes a professor at the Massachusetts Institute of Technology

2012 *Time* magazine names Sara 1 of the 25 most important space scientists

2013 Sara wins the MacArthur Foundation "genius" grant

2017 NASA begins Sara's TESS Project to find new exoplanets

Sara wants more young women to study science.

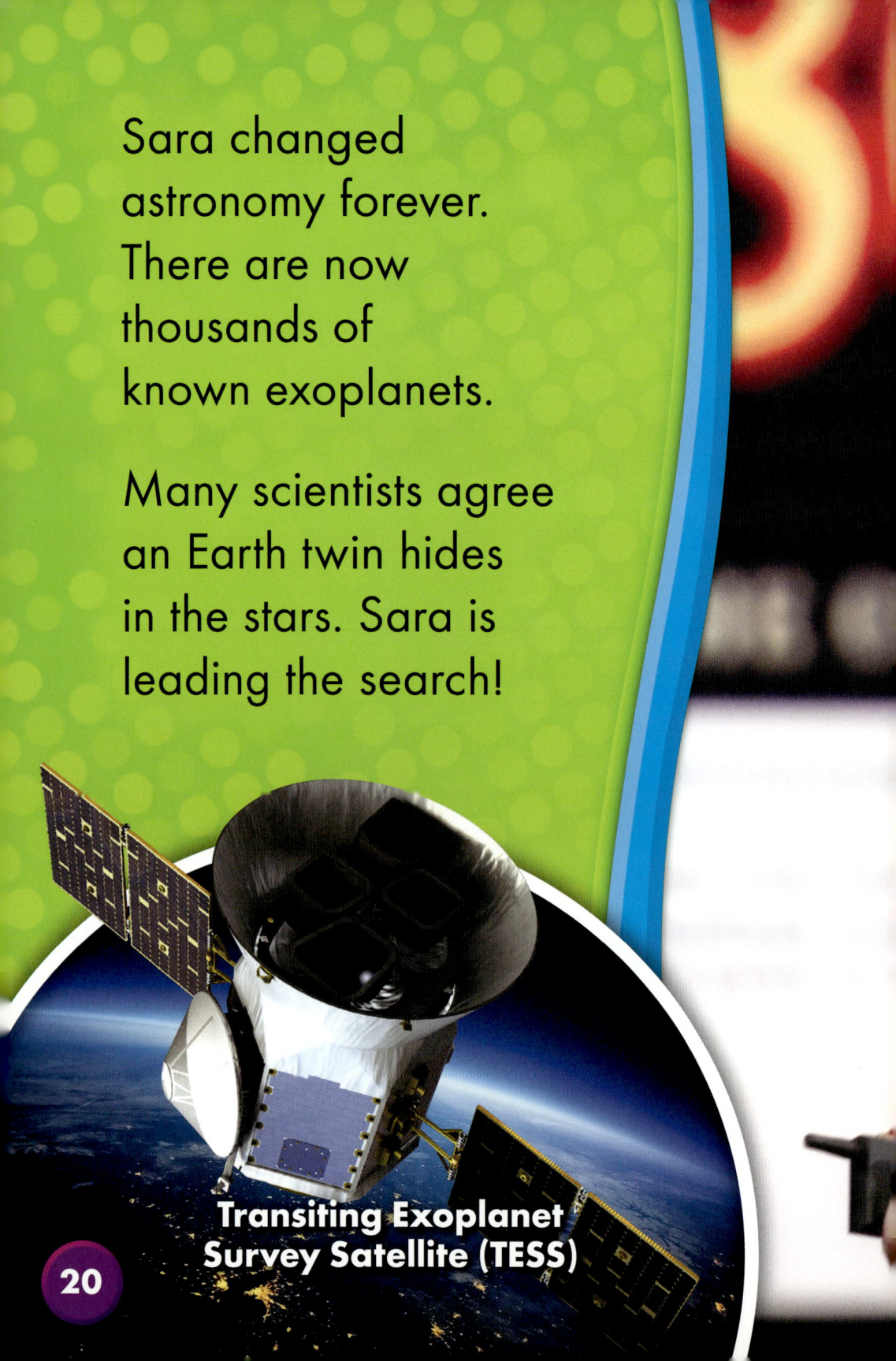

Sara changed astronomy forever. There are now thousands of known exoplanets.

Many scientists agree an Earth twin hides in the stars. Sara is leading the search!

Transiting Exoplanet Survey Satellite (TESS)

"I ALWAYS FEEL LIKE MY BEST ACCOMPLISHMENTS ARE IN THE FUTURE. THAT'S WHAT KEEPS ME GOING. **THE FUTURE IS ALWAYS BETTER."**
(2017)

Glossary

amazed—feeling a lot of surprise

astronomy—the scientific study of stars, planets, and other objects in outer space

divorced—separated and stopped being married

exoplanets—planets that circle around a star other than the Sun

grant—an amount of money that is given to someone to be used for a certain purpose

NASA—a group in the United States that does space travel and research; NASA stands for National Aeronautics and Space Administration.

outer space—the area outside of Earth where there are stars and planets

professor—a teacher at a college

scientist—a person who is trained in science and whose job involves doing research or solving scientific problems

support—to keep something going

To Learn More

AT THE LIBRARY

Feldman, Thea. *Katherine Johnson*. New York, N.Y.: Simon Spotlight, 2017.

Robbins, Dean. *Margaret and the Moon: How Margaret Hamilton Saved the First Lunar Landing*. New York, N.Y.: Alfred A. Knopf, 2017.

Swatling, Todd. *What Happens to Space Probes?* New York, N.Y.: 2019.

ON THE WEB

FACTSURFER

Factsurfer.com gives you a safe, fun way to find more information.

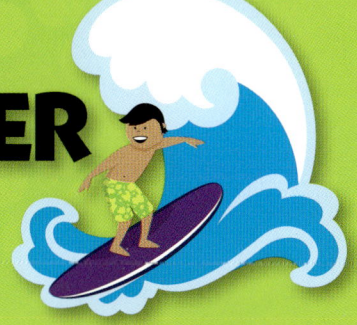

1. Go to www.factsurfer.com.

2. Enter "Sara Seager" into the search box.

3. Click the "Surf" button and select your book cover to see a list of related web sites.

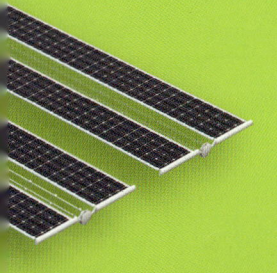

Index

astronomy, 8, 20
Canada, 6, 7
Earth, 4, 20
exoplanets, 4, 12, 14, 16, 18, 20
family, 6, 7, 16, 17
friends, 7
grant, 17
NASA, 14, 15, 18
outer space, 4
parents, 6, 10
professor, 18
profile, 9
quotes, 5, 11, 21
school, 10, 12
science, 19
scientist, 4, 10, 20
stars, 9, 20

teacher, 13
timeline, 19
United States, 10

The images in this book are reproduced through the courtesy of: Maarten de Boer, front cover (Sara); Alan Uster, front cover (Earth/moon); NASA Image Collection, front cover (exoplanet), pp. 8, 9; Nerthuz, p. 3; NASA Goddard, p. 4 (inset); MacArthur Foundation, pp. 4-5, 10 (inset); The Washington Post, pp. 6-7; Richard Shotwell/Invision/AP, pp. 10-11; NASA/JPL-Caltech, pp. 12-13 (top left), 16; NASA/Bill Ingalls, p. 13 (bottom right); NASA/Tony Gray, p. 14 (inset); Zhukova Valentyna, pp. 14-15; Bennett Raglin, pp. 16-17 (top right); Ivy Photos, pp. 18-19; Associated Press, p. 20 (inset); Bret Hartman/TED, pp. 20-21; Nerthuz, p. 22.